W9-BAG-554

In John 8:44 we read that Satan is a liar and that he "does not stand in the truth." In her book, Lori Strong describes a process of praying for people by "painting" a circle of truth around them using the Word of God. When she exercises authority through prayer within that circle of truth, she reminds Satan that he cannot stand within that circle of truth. When the Word of God is used in this fashion, like a sword, it removes Satan's jurisdiction and he falls! I heartily endorse Lori's book for those who have a heart to see afflicted people set free from bondage.

RICK HEEREN, VICE PRESIDENT
MIDWEST REGION, HARVEST EVANGELISM, INC.
AUTHOR, *THANK GOD IT'S MONDAY!*

When you are in trouble, you need help and you need it fast; it must be practical and from someone who knows what they are talking about. Lori Strong knows what she is talking about; she is very practical with her advice and has written a book that is simple, scripturally sound and easy to use. I recommend this book for the hurting and those who work with the hurting.

RICH MARSHALL
AUTHOR: *GOD@WORK*

This book is a practical, insightful guide for individuals and their families to break generational curses that have taken root in their lives and to fully embrace the abundant life Christ promises in the Bible. We believe that many people will find total spiritual freedom through this work, and we pray that it will find its way into the hands of everyone who needs it.

DENNIS AND MEGAN DOYLE
CO-FOUNDERS OF NEHEMIAH PARTNERS
CONTRIBUTING AUTHORS: *GOD@WORK*
AND *WOMEN OF DESTINY BIBLE*

TAKE UP THE Sword of The Spirit

CRUSHING CURSES WITH THE WORD OF GOD

Lori Strong

CREATION
HOUSE PRESS
A STRANG COMPANY

TAKE UP THE SWORD OF THE SPIRIT by Lori Strong
Published by Creation House Press
A Strang Company
600 Rinehart Road
Lake Mary, FL 32746
www.creationhouse.com

This book or parts thereof may not be reproduced in any
form, stored in a retrieval system or transmitted in any form
by any means—electronic, mechanical, photocopy, recording
or otherwise—without prior written permission of the publishers, except as provided by United States of America copyright law.

Unless otherwise noted, the Scripture quotations are from
the New King James Version of the Bible. Copyright ©
1979, 1980, 1982 by Thomas Nelson, Inc., publishers. Used
by permission.

Scripture quotations marked NIV are from the Holy Bible,
New International Version. Copyright © 1973, 1978, 1984,
International Bible Society. Used by permission.

Scripture quotations marked NLT are from the Holy Bible,
New Living Translation, copyright © 1996. Used by permis-
sion of Tyndale House Publishers, Inc., Wheaton, IL 60189.
All rights reserved.

Cover design by Terry Clifton

Copyright © 2003 by Lori Strong

All rights reserved

Library of Congress Control Number: 2003108623

International Standard Book Number: 1-59185-278-1

03 04 05 06   8 7 6 5 4 3 2 1
Printed in the United States of America

I dedicate this book to my dad who endured the results of the curses, yet came out at the other side in glory with Jesus. In March 2002, he received the blessing of receiving Jesus as Lord in his heart and is now rejoicing in heaven. I thank God that I was able to use the Word to break the curses that so long affected my relationship with him. I encourage you, the reader, to experience the power of the Word in your family before those you love leave this earth. There is peace and joy in knowing that the Word can break curses and bring blessings to all your relationships. I thank my husband, Paul, for encouraging me to follow the leading of the Holy Spirit and write this book. To my daughter Tasha, thank you for praying every week for me as I went to the office and wrote until it was finished. Thank you, my boys, Isaiah, Josiah and Joshua, for smiling and sending me off on this great journey.

CONTENTS

Foreword

L ori Strong is one of God's special servants. Lori and her husband Paul are devout disciples of Christ who unlike many young leaders today understand and model pure religion. (See James 1:27.) The Strong family is refreshing in this season where so many ministers are seeking to emulate popular glamorous ministries not based on the teachings and lifestyle of Christ. The primary theme of Christ's earthly ministry was to bring the Good News of God's love to the least, the lost and hurting. We live in a culture and society where the need for effective pure religion and ministry reflecting the spirit of Christ to the hurting is critical.

After pastoring several local churches for many years, preaching nationally and providing spiritual counsel to Christian leaders, I have seen the devastating effects of strongholds and bondage in the lives of seekers and believers. Husbands and wives, children and seniors often struggle for years to make sense and overcome the trauma of abuse and hurt still haunting them. Even pastors and ministers are impacted by satanic schemes designed by the forces of darkness to stagger and stagnate the advance of the kingdom of God and the abundant life found in Christ. That's why this book is so important and relevant for the body of Christ and the community at large.

Lori and Paul's ministry with young incarcerated women and men gives them the hands-on insight to move Christians to the next level of dealing with those weights that beset so many. (See Hebrews 12:1.) Lori is an evangelistic teacher with a shepherd's and prophetic intercessor's heart. Her own testimony of deliverance and journey towards wholeness is an exciting example of the power of prayer and biblical discipleship.

Deliverance ministry is widely misunderstood today. The biblical text paints a picture of a journey from captivity to freedom. Deliverance is proactive and not simply reactive. Yet, so many people flock to church altars Sunday after Sunday to receive prayers for deliverance without a clear vision for the next step.

The good news is that Christian leaders are finally beginning to recognize that healthy deliverance will involve prayer for spiritual breakthrough, counseling and biblical instruction.

The principles and curriculum contained within are what I call "deliverance discipleship." The essence of genuine biblical discipleship is summarized in the New Testament Book of Ephesians as equipping the saints to do the work of the ministry. (See Ephesians 4:12.) The term equip has a deeper meaning beyond the conventional concept of it as a synonym for teaching. The broader meaning of equipping includes a major focus on healing and training. So then true biblical ministry begins with healing the hurting. The church often seeks to train people in righteousness before basic issues are resolved in the lives of these young believers. This book will help advance a new ministry paradigm through "deliverance discipleship."

This resource was born in the crucible of trials, tribulations and triumphs. Those with a discerning heart will sense the longing and underlying travail of spirit that resonates beneath the text. Here is a practitioner's testament of hope for the hurting. This is no theoretical hogwash steeped in academic mumbo jumbo. It is a clear, concise practical guidebook for shepherds and disciples. It is a rare gift to effectively simplify the profound. This book succeeds in reflecting this gifting but also excels in offering a glimmer of hope and new lifestyle to those struggling with issues that haunt them and their quality of life.

May God transform your life and empower you to impact the lives of others through *Take Up the Sword of the Spirit: Crushing Curses With the Word of God.*

—DR. MARK POLLARD
PRESIDENT, THE COMMON GROUND COALITION
CHAIRMAN, THE CRUSADE FOR SPIRITUAL AWAKENING
ATLANTA, GEORGIA

Introduction

There's an old saying that reads, "As the twig is bent, so grows the tree." It implies that the way we are raised—or "bent"—is the way we are destined to turn out in life. Well, praise God, it does not have to be that way, but we do need to do some things to correct our "bent" lives. We know that the Word of God states that "faith without works is dead" (James 2:26), so let's get busy!

There are several ways to read this book and receive what you need from it for your life. The first thing to note is that my Father in heaven is the expert who directed me to share with you how you can be released from the bondage of your past, your parents' past, and your grandparents' past, so please look at the message, not the messenger.

Secondly, note that everyone has an individual way of praying to God. The prayers included in this book are to assist you in the direction of blessing your life, marriage and relationships with others. I encourage you to seek God for how you can use His Word to pray for what you desire. Remember, "whatever things you ask in prayer, believing, you will receive" (Matthew 21:22). It's not important whether we sit, kneel or stand while praying or whether or not we use King James English in our prayers. The most important thing is that we pray!

Lastly, I encourage you to seek the Lord in all areas of your life that may have been affected by the generations before you. Sometimes we don't see what may be obvious until we seek the Lord with humility and with a willingness to change. This book is a tool to show you how to use the Word of God to break generational curses, but it is not the only way to do so. If you have an issue that has affected your life in a negative way, you may need to seek spiritual counsel through a pastor or a Christian counselor for healing and deliverance. Remember, the Word of God states that we should seek godly counsel. This book may help identify some areas in your life that need to be addressed, and a counselor can help you work through them.

My request is that you don't skip over a chapter because you think it doesn't apply. It's wise to pray the prayer to cover every area that may have been cursed in prior generations that you may not know about.

"For we ourselves were also once foolish, disobedient, deceived, serving various lusts and pleasures, living in malice and envy, hateful and hating one another. But when the kindness and love of God our Savior toward man appeared, not by works of righteousness which we have done, but according to His mercy He saved us, through the washing of regeneration and renewing of the Holy Spirit, whom He poured out on us abundantly through Jesus Christ our Savior, that having been justified by His grace we should become heirs according to the hope of eternal life" (Titus 3: 3–7).

I pray that as you read, the Lord will richly bless you as you submit your heart to Him. May your life be touched and changed by the power of God's Word, in Jesus name. Amen.

CHAPTER 1

Generational Curses Defined

My husband and I have been ministering in prisons for the last eight years. We have seen many types of people who have committed a variety of offenses. We teach parenting and we have seen all styles of parenting and many people who have not been taught how to parent their children. We tend to practice what we have learned. Those who don't hear the words "I love you" while growing up usually don't say "I love you" to their children (although there are exceptions, including some who go to extremes to make up for what their parents didn't offer them). The difficulty we see most consistently throughout the prison population is the existence of generational curses. Many examples come to mind. At one time, there were three mother-daughter pairs of inmates. They either committed a crime together or were involved with different crimes but were incarcerated simultaneously. There also have been many cousins, aunts, nieces and sisters in prison at the same time. For many families that seem plagued with generational curses, there seems to be a revolving door into prison. This is devastating to me! We need to help them break the generational curse at their generation. To do this, we must first love them and build trusting relationships with them. Many of the women and men in the prisons that we go into have children of all ages. What will happen to these children if the inmates fail to change their lifestyles and attitudes?

That is why we need a book on generational curses and blessings. Your situation may not seem as devastating as the one these inmate parents and their children face, but any curse is devastating if it is not stopped.

Another example of generational curses in the prison population was a 21-year-old mother of a 2-year-old. She was raised in a home where getting high was normal and still is. Her daughter is at this home and the mother is fine with that. She thinks it is the norm to get high. Now we are dealing with a three-generation curse. She, her parents and her daughter will all go on believing it is normal to get high unless the curse is stopped.

Another very common example of generational curses in family lines is abuse. Approximately 80 percent of the women in our parenting groups have been sexually, physically and/or emotionally abused by one of their parents. They go on to be abused by their partners. Then their children see the abuse and either become perpetrators and/or victims. This pattern needs to stop somewhere in the family line. The only thing that can stop it forever is the Word of God!

To Be Blessed and to Be Cursed; What Does That Mean?

According to the world, blessing means to have things, both material and spiritual. For example, we often respond to the question, "How are you?" by stating, "I'm blessed." How often does someone answer that same question with "I'm cursed"? It would be rare to hear such a response.

With this in mind, why do we operate in our daily lives as if we are cursed? We allow so many of the generational curses from the third and fourth generations to continue to penetrate our daily lives and especially our marriages without even knowing it is happening.

To understand how our lives have been cursed or blessed, we need to understand the meaning of several words. Depending on the authority used, there are many definitions of cursing and blessing, as you will see below:

Webster's Dictionary definition:[1]
Blessed: joyful, healing, happy and favored.
To bless: to invoke God's favor upon, to bestow happiness or prosperity upon.
Cursed: deserving a curse, detestable, a source of calamity or evil.
To curse: to invoke evil or injury upon, to damn.

The world's definition:
Blessed: to have possessions, to have happiness and to be prosperous.
To bless: to give someone something they do not have, to do favors for.
Cursed: to walk in destruction, to be poor, to have nothing; everything you do fails.
To curse: to bring death and destruction on something or someone.

The Word's definition:
Blessed: to have increase, to have God open His treasures, to be the lender and not the borrower, to have your soul prosper. (See Philippians 4:19; Proverbs 22:7; 3 John 2.)
To bless: to give in abundance, to be gracious to. (See Ephesians 3:20; Numbers 6:25b.)

3

Cursed: to have no increase. (See Deuteronomy 28:18.)

To curse: to destroy. (See Deuteronomy 28:20.)

By studying these definitions you will begin to get the idea of why we need to receive blessings that have been promised to us and cast out the curses from which we have been delivered. You may ask "what blessings have I been promised?" and "what curses do I need to be delivered from?" Let's go to the Word of God and see what God has told us from the beginning of time.

Within the first two pages of the Bible, both blessings and curses are mentioned. Obviously these topics are important to God and therefore should be important for us to understand in relation to our lives.

In the very first chapter of the Bible the Lord begins to speak of blessings. In reference to His creation of male and female it says, "God blessed them" (Genesis 1:28). In the second chapter He warns Adam and Eve that they will be cursed if they eat "of the tree of the knowledge of good and evil" (Genesis 2:17).

We could go through the entire Bible and find many areas in which blessings and curses are mentioned and sometimes taught in great detail. As a matter of fact, the words "blessing," "blessed" and "bless" are listed 496 times in the Bible. The words "cursed," "curse" and "curses" are listed 173 times in the Bible. This tells us a couple of things. First, the Lord allows us to be blessed or cursed based on our obedience to Him and His Word. Second, the Lord wants to bless us much more than He wants to curse us.

Evidence of Generational Curses
From the Beginning

The first people to be cursed in the Bible were Adam and Eve. Through their disobedience, they were cursed by God and banned from the Tree of Life and the Garden of Eden. They had two sons, Cain and Abel, and passed the generational curse

4

down to them. God cursed Cain for killing his brother. "When you till the ground, it shall no longer yield its strength to you. A fugitive and a vagabond you shall be on the earth" (Genesis 4:12). This curse was the curse of lack. Then we read on in Genesis about the genealogy of Adam's family. All of the children that were born into the following generations were cursed due to Adam's sin. Genesis 6:5–6 sums it up for us: "Then the Lord saw that the wickedness of man was great in the earth, and that every intent of the thoughts of his heart was only evil continually. And the Lord was sorry that He had made man on the earth, and He was grieved in His heart."

Can you imagine God saying that He is sorry that He made you? That's how He looked upon Adam and all his descendants until Noah. When generations are full of sin and no one takes responsibility to stop it, it is a curse. I know that I want the Lord to never have reason to say He is sorry He made me. I want Him to be pleased with all my ways.

So the Lord destroyed all of the living creatures that He had created up until Noah and his family.

Evidence of Generational Blessings in the Word

Why did God allow Noah to live? It is because Noah was righteous before God. (See Genesis 7:1.) Why did God allow the rest of the generations to live? It is because He made a covenant that He "will never again curse the ground for man's sake" (Genesis 8:21).

The first person to receive a blessing and maintain it in the Bible was Noah. Because Noah and his sons exercised faith and obeyed God, Genesis 9:1 states that God blessed Noah and his sons. Faith and obedience to God cannot be separated. You must believe God exists before you can please Him by doing His will. The following scriptures lay this out clearly:

> By faith we understand that the worlds were framed by the word of God, so that the things which are seen were not made of things which are visible.
> But without faith it is impossible to please Him,

5

for he who comes to God must believe that He is, and that He is a rewarder of those who diligently seek Him.

—HEBREWS 11:3, 6

We know that faith and obedience were the keys to blessings from God as the following scriptures indicate:

By faith Noah, being divinely warned of things not yet seen, moved with godly fear, prepared an ark for the saving of his household, by which he condemned the world and became heir of the righteousness which is according to faith.

—HEBREWS 11:7

By faith Abraham obeyed when he was called to go out to the place which he would receive as an inheritance. And he went out, not knowing where he was going.

—HEBREWS 11:8

By faith Sarah herself also received strength to conceive seed, and she bore a child when she was past the age, because she judged Him faithful who had promised.

—HEBREWS 11:11

These heroes of faith not only received blessings on earth, but also are receiving their ultimate blessing in heaven.

But now they desire a better, that is, a heavenly country. Therefore God is not ashamed to be called their God, for He has prepared a city for them.

—HEBREWS 11:16

By faith and through our obedience, we can receive blessings. God blessed Abraham according to his obedience. Genesis 12:1–3 states:

> Now the Lord had said to Abram: "Get out of your country, from your family and from your father's house, to a land that I will show you. I will make you a great nation; I will bless you and make your name great; and you shall be a blessing. I will bless those who bless you, and I will curse him who curses you; and in you all the families of the earth shall be blessed."

Yet, as we know, Abram took his nephew Lot with him. We see that the Lord did not fully bless him until he was completely in obedience to God. Abram told Lot:

> Please let there be no strife between you and me, and between my herdsmen and your herdsmen; for we are brethren. Is not the whole land before you? Please separate from me. If you take the left, then I will go to the right; or, if you go to the right, then I will go to the left.
>
> —GENESIS 13:8–9

When Abram had faithfully told Lot to leave (as the Lord instructed him to leave his "family") then the Lord was able to bless him to the fullness of blessings.

> And the Lord said to Abram, after Lot had separated from him: "Lift your eyes now and look from the place where you are—northward, southward, eastward, and westward; for all the land which you see I give to you and your descendants forever."
>
> —GENESIS 13: 14–15

This is the evidence of generational blessings. God not only blessed Abram, but also his seed. In the same way that curses can pass down from the third and fourth generations, so can blessings! Which do you want to pass down to your children, grandchildren and great grandchildren?

The key to maintaining your blessing is faith and obedience!

What is the difference between sin and iniquity?

Cindy Jacobs answers this question in her book, *The Voice of God*, "Sin is basically the cause and iniquity includes the effect."[2] Generational iniquities that bring on generational curses work something like this: A parent commits adultery and does not repent for it. This sin produces a generational iniquity that is passed down the family lineage. Although the children and adults in this family do not commit adultery, they are living with an iniquity that may be present and not bound until prayer and the use of God's Word crush it.

The problem is that a lot of us do not know that the iniquity and sin were ever committed by past generations. Therefore we live with the bondage of iniquity and curse without needing to. Prior to prayer and repentance, we should identify the sins and iniquities of our forefathers. You may wonder how to do that. I believe that through the covering of every area of sin and iniquity listed in the following chapters, you will have included many areas of generational sin without having to go back to talk to grandma, great grandma and so on. In fact, sometimes it is impossible to do so because these family members are deceased.

How can there be generational curses if I believe that Jesus died for my sins on the cross?

We know that when Jesus died on the cross for our sins, He also died for the curses that plague us today. Just as we are to repent for our sins so we will not perish, we must do something to cast these curses out of our lives to never return again. (See Luke 13:3.)

You may think that Jesus already did that for you when He died on the cross. Yes, He did, but He clearly states that we must do our part too. We must believe that He died to free us from these curses and that we can use His Word to reject the curses we have received into our lives, knowingly or unknowingly.

The Word states that faith without works is dead. If you believe that Jesus died on the cross for the curses that plague you today, then you must not only believe, but you also must act on your faith. If you simply say that you don't have to do anything to be saved or delivered from the generational curses in your family, then you are like the example James writes about in James 2: 14–24 (NLT).

> Dear brothers and sisters, what's the use of saying you have faith if you don't prove it by your actions? That kind of faith can't save anyone. Suppose you see a brother or sister who needs food or clothing, and you say, "Well, good-bye and God bless you; stay warm and eat well"—but then you don't give that person any food or clothing. What good does that do?
>
> So you see, it isn't enough just to have faith. Faith that doesn't show itself by good deeds is no faith at all—it is dead and useless.
>
> Now someone may argue, "Some people have faith; others have good deeds." I say, "I can't see your faith if you don't have good deeds, but I will show you my faith through my good deeds."
>
> Do you still think it's enough just to believe that there is one God? Well, even the demons believe this, and they tremble in terror! Fool! When will you ever learn that faith that does not result in good deeds is useless?
>
> Don't you remember that our ancestor Abraham was declared right with God because of what he did when he offered his son Isaac on the altar? You see, he was trusting God so much that he was willing to do whatever God told him to do. His faith was made complete by what he did—by his actions. And so it happened just as the Scriptures say: "Abraham believed God, so God declared him to be righteous." He was even called "the friend of God." So you see, we are made right with God by what we do, not by faith alone.

It takes faith to believe God's Word will break generational curses in our families, but it takes the act of applying His Word in our lives to fulfill the "works" that bring life.

If we believe that Jesus died for our sins and we do not use the Word of God in our lives, then Jesus died in vain.

The Use of the Two-Edged Sword

Hebrews 4:12 states: "For the word of God is living and powerful, and sharper than any two-edged sword, piercing even the division of soul and spirit, and of joints and marrow, and is a discerner of the thoughts and intents of the heart."

According to this description of the Word, it must also be used as the way to cast out those things in our lives that have caused division, bondage and destruction. It's time we used the two-edged sword as the weapon that God created it to be.

Matthew 11:28–30 is an invitation from Jesus to:

> Come to Me, all you who labor and are heavy laden, and I will give you rest. Take My yoke upon you and learn from Me, for I am gentle and lowly in heart, and you will find rest for your souls. For My yoke is easy and My burden is light.

Putting the Word to Use in Your Life

The remainder of this book will detail generational curses that plague marriages and other relationships. These curses will be explained in a life example intended to help you see where curses may be in your life or in the generations prior to yours. Then we come to the blessing that is always the opposite of the curse listed. Finally, you will be referred to the scriptures that apply to this blessing and that will lead you to pray blessings against these curses that may have come down from the third or even fourth generations in your family. Several prayers are included because the more we pray God's Word, the more power our words have. The more we hear what we are saying, the more we will believe; our "faith comes by hearing, and hearing by the word of God" (Romans 10:17). This is how the two-edged sword will divide the curse from the blessing and expose what we can have in our lives and our marriages.

Remember, Jesus died on the cross for these curses to be cast into the sea of forgetfulness. Why are we living as if He never did this for us, but still call ourselves doers of the Word of God?

Let not His death on the cross be in vain any longer!

Everyone has his individual way of talking to God. Please remember that these are just guides. The best way to pray is the way you know how, always being led by the Holy Spirit.

---

1 William Morris, ed., et al., *Webster's Comprehensive Dictionary: Encyclopedic Edition* (Chicago: Ferguson Publishing, 2000).

2 Cindy Jacobs, *The Voice of God* (Ventura, CA: Regal Books, 1997).

CHAPTER 2

Lack of Faith and Trust

CURSE: Lack of belief in God

LIFE EXAMPLE: Jessica grew up in a family where her mom and dad dropped her off at church every Sunday but did not come in to hear the teaching. She knew that there was a God because that is what her pastor had taught in church. Her mom was the type of person who didn't believe anything until she saw it. Therefore, when Jessica would come out of church all excited and share with her mom about what she had learned, her mom would say, "How could you believe in a God you cannot see?" Jessica became discouraged and eventually quit attending church. In her heart she knew that God existed, but she was not being taught the same thing at home as she was at church.

Eventually Jessica moved out of her home and went to college. It was there that she met her husband to be. Mark had been involved in church all of his life, and he attempted to persuade Jessica to attend, but she refused time and time again. The day that they got married was the first time Jessica had been to church since she was fifteen years old. After their wedding, she did not attend church again. Mark struggled with this until he went to see his pastor. His pastor encouraged him to pray for Jessica daily. He also told Mark that it would be wise to stop inviting Jessica to church and continue to be the godly husband he was meant to be. When Mark and Jessica had their first son a year after their wedding, Mark decided that he would begin to take the baby to church with him every Sunday. Jessica objected strongly to this, but Mark won the argument and Samuel began to attend church from the time he was six weeks old. When Samuel turned two and a half, he came home from church and began to share with his mom about God and what he had learned in church. She instantly replied, "How can you believe in a God you cannot see?" Almost as soon as those words came out of her mouth, she realized whom she sounded like. She also realized that she was doing to her son what her mother had done to her. Not even a week passed before Jessica was back in church praying that the Lord would break any curse of disbelief in God that ran through the generations in her family.

CURSE: Lack of belief in God

BLESSING: Belief that God is sovereign and experiencing the peace and joy that go with the belief.

SCRIPTURE:

> But without faith it is impossible to please Him, for he who comes to God must believe that He is, and that He is a rewarder of those who diligently seek Him.
>
> —HEBREWS 11:6

Prayer:

Father, in the name of Your Son, Jesus, I thank You that Your Word says that I must have faith and believe that You are God in order to please You. Lord, I desire to please You. I break any curse of disbelief in You from my parents' generation, their parents' generation and the generations following me. I thank You that You will reward me as I diligently seek You. I believe in You, Lord, and nothing will stop me from believing that You are God. Amen.

Scripture:

In this you greatly rejoice, though now for a little while, if need be, you have been grieved by various trials, that the genuineness of your faith, being much more precious than gold that perishes, though it is tested by fire, may be found to praise, honor, and glory at the revelation of Jesus Christ, whom having not seen you love. Though now you do not see Him, yet believing, you rejoice with joy inexpressible and full of glory, receiving the end of your faith—the salvation of your souls.

—1 Peter 1:6–9

Prayer:

Father, I thank You for Your Son, Jesus, whom I can believe and love although I have not seen Him. Thank You, Lord, for giving me a measure of faith so I can pass it down to my children and their children and the generations following them. I break the curse of disbelief in You, Lord, from my parent's generation and their parent's generation. I believe that You, Lord, are the only God and that Your Son, Jesus, died on the cross for me. I rejoice, as Your Word states, receiving the end of my faith, which is the salvation of my soul. I believe and receive that You are God over all and I believe that You can do all things in my life. Amen.

CURSE: Fear of man

LIFE EXAMPLE: I grew up thinking that everything I did should be pleasing to my mom. I didn't know the difference between pleasing and respecting. I thought that if I did or believed anything against what my mom believed, she would not love me anymore. I aimed to please my mom, but my sister aimed to please everyone. We learned this because as we were growing up, if we said anything that did not agree with our mother, we would feel horrible. This continued through most of my teen years and into my twenties. I was delivered from this when I received Christ into my life. That was probably the most displeasing thing I had ever done according to my mother, so anything else I did that did not line up with her beliefs did not surprise her. My sister, at age forty, has just begun to stop trying to please everyone. People pleasers are not born that way, but most of the time become that way in the early part of their lives. They continue in that pattern until they get tired of trying to please man who will never be pleased anyway. My daughter is ten years old and we have recognized some people-pleasing qualities in her life. We pray and teach her that her goal should be to please God in all that she does. I have seen in the last year that she is much more focused on God pleasing than people pleasing. We encourage leadership in our children and reverence to God no matter what man thinks. This model of parenting is one way that the curse of being fearful of man will be broken. I encourage parents to direct their children to please God, not mom and dad. Then the Word of God can be their guide for the rest of their lives.

CURSE: Fear of man

BLESSING: Fear (reverence) of God

SCRIPTURE:

The LORD is my light and my salvation; whom shall I fear? The Lord is the strength of my life; of whom shall I be afraid?

—PSALM 27:1

PRAYER:

Father, in the name of Your Son, Jesus, I thank You that I need not fear man. You are my light and salvation. Through You all things happen, so I will not have a fear of man. I break the curse of fear of man in my life and my children's lives. I thank You, Lord that You are the strength of my life and I can be confident and stand upright before man without being fearful of him. Amen.

SCRIPTURE:

Let your conduct be without covetousness; be content with such things as you have. For He Himself has said, "I will never leave you nor forsake you." So we may boldly say: "The Lord is my helper; I will not fear. What can man do to me?"

—HEBREWS 13: 5–6

PRAYER:

Father, in the name of Your Son, Jesus, I thank You for being my helper in times of need and despair. I thank You that I have no fear of what man thinks of me or my behavior. I pray, Lord, that You will direct my ways, and that man can do nothing to me. I aim to please You, Lord. I break the curses over my life and the lives of my family members of man pleasing and fear of what man might think. I commit to having a reverence for You only, Lord. Amen.

SCRIPTURE:

For God has not given us a spirit of fear, but of power and of love and of a sound mind.

—2 TIMOTHY 1:7

PRAYER:

Father, in the name of Your Son, Jesus, I thank You for giving me a spirit of power and of love and of a sound mind. I thank You, Lord that I fear nothing that man may do to me, but I aim to please only You in my thoughts and behavior. I thank You that you have not given me a spirit of fear, and that I can walk freely from any fear of man in my life, my children's lives and my grandchildrens' lives. Thank You, Lord, for peace that flows down to the second, third and fourth generations. Amen.

Chapter 3

Problems in Marriage

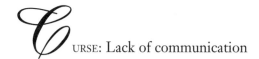URSE: Lack of communication

LIFE EXAMPLE: John grew up with a dad who was very controlling in the home. Whatever John's father said was the final word. John and his siblings never could express how they felt, or they would be punished. John grew up learning to walk away from conflict and to shut down during serious conversations with his wife. When John's wife wants to talk things out and get to the bottom of a matter, John shuts down and walks out.

John has a difficult time handling conflict because he was never taught how to communicate and resolve misunderstandings or disagreements. John's dad had grown up in a home just like the home that he became the head of. Already experiencing a curse to the third generation in his family, if John does not break the curse in his family, it will continue to flow down to his children and so forth through the generations.

CURSE: Lack of communication

BLESSING: Great relationships with excellent communication and ability to express feelings

SCRIPTURE:

> Do not withhold good from those to whom it is due, when it is in the power of your hand to do so. Do not say to your neighbor, "Go, and come back, and tomorrow I will give it," when you have it with you.
> —PROVERBS 3:27–28

PRAYER:

> *Father, in the name of Your Son, Jesus, I bind the curse of lack of communication from the generations before me. I will not withhold my feelings in the relationships in my family. I will have excellent communication with my family and I will express my feelings appropriately so conflict will not build up in my home. Thank You for giving me the ability to share my feelings at appropriate times, not too late and not too early. Amen.*

SCRIPTURE:

> Be kindly affectionate to one another in brotherly love, in honor giving preference to one another; not lagging in diligence, fervent in spirit, serving the Lord; rejoicing in hope, patient in tribulation, continuing steadfastly in prayer; distributing to the needs of the saints, given to hospitality.
> Bless those who persecute you; bless and do not curse. Rejoice with those who rejoice, and weep with those who weep. Be of the same mind toward

one another. Do not set your mind on high things, but associate with the humble. Do not be wise in your own opinion.

Repay no one evil for evil. Have regard for good things in the sight of all men. If it is possible, as much as depends on you, live peaceably with all men.

—ROMANS 12:10–18

PRAYER:

Father, in the name of Your Son, Jesus, I thank You for Your command to rejoice and weep with the members of my family. I pray that You would help us be of the same mind toward one another, communicating with one another. I bind the curse over our family of shutting down our feelings and having a lack of communication. I release peaceful communication and openness in our family relationships. I thank You, Lord, that I can bless my family members through open communication, and not curse them. I pray that we can live out this scripture in our hearts and our lives. Amen.

CURSE: Lack of affection in marriage

LIFE EXAMPLE: Greg was raised in a home where everyone was openly affectionate, and if you walked into their house and didn't give his mom a hug she would grab you and hug you, even if it was your first time visiting. When Greg met Alicia he knew that they were going to be married. He loved the fact that she was affectionate and loving like his family was, but when they got married, this all changed. She became distant and would not hug or kiss him in public or hold his hand. When they were in their home, she would jump if he touched her. Greg was very troubled by this, and they had many arguments regarding Alicia's lack of affection. She said it was because her family never showed affection, and she wasn't comfortable with it. Greg was confused because he felt like she lied to him because she was affectionate before they got married. She also said that many men had sexually abused her in her family, and she did not like to be touched unless she initiated it. Greg was hurt and unsure of what to do. He continued to give her hugs and let her know how much he loved her. He felt like it was a breakthrough when she was willing to hold his hand in public. The little accomplishments are great, and they will lead to a breakthrough in this generational curse as he prays God's Word over this situation and believes that God will meet all his needs. This curse is also detrimental to their children because children need to see their parents love each other, and affection is one of the most obvious displays of love.

CURSE: Lack of affection in marriage

BLESSINGS: Frequent displays of affection and love in marriage

SCRIPTURE:

> Let the husband render to his wife the affection due her, and likewise also the wife to her husband.
> —1 CORINTHIANS 7:3

PRAYER:

> *Father, in the name of Your Son, Jesus, I thank You for an affectionate spouse who obeys Your Word. I break the generational curse of lack of affection, in the name of Jesus. I believe that Your Word is true, and I will render to my spouse the affection due to him/her. I break the curse of unmet needs in marriage from past generations in my family and in the generations to follow. I believe that my children will have affectionate spouses and that all their needs will be met. Amen.*

Scripture:

Let love be without hypocrisy. Abhor what is evil. Cling to what is good. Be kindly affectionate to one another with brotherly love, in honor giving preference to one another; not lagging in diligence, fervent in spirit, serving the Lord; rejoicing in hope, patient in tribulation, continuing steadfastly in prayer.

—Romans 12:9–12

Prayer:

Father, in the name of Your Son, Jesus, I thank You that I can rely on Your Word for guidance in my marriage. I will be diligent and rejoice in the hope that my marriage will be one that glorifies You, Lord. I will be patient even when I have not seen results. I will continue to pray and believe that Your Word can restore anything that the enemy has stolen. I break the curse of lack of affection in marriages from past generations and the ones to follow. I will cling to those things that are good and I will be affectionate to my spouse no matter what. Amen.

Scripture:

Husbands, love your wives, just as Christ also loved the church and gave Himself for her, that He might sanctify and cleanse her with the washing of water by the word, that He might present her to Himself a glorious church, not having spot or wrinkle or any such thing, but that she should be holy and without blemish. So husbands ought to love their own wives as their own bodies; he who loves his wife loves himself. For no one ever hated his own flesh, but nourishes and cherishes it, just as the Lord does the church.

—Ephesians 5:25–29

PRAYER:

Father in the name of Your Son, Jesus, I thank You for breaking the curse of unmet physical needs in my marriage. Thank You for giving me a perfect example in Christ of how to love my spouse. I will love my spouse as You love the church, and I will nourish and cherish him/her. I break the curse of lack of affection in the generations before mine and those to follow. Amen.

CURSE: Adultery

LIFE EXAMPLE: Pat grew up in a family where it was "cool" to "sleep around" even if you were married. Susan also had some adultery in her family while growing up. So, when Pat and Susan got married, there was unfaithfulness from the beginning. Pat was the first to commit adultery, and when Susan found out she thought she would do the same to Pat. This went back and forth until finally they decided to make a change in their marriage. They both received counseling for a period of time and then recommitted themselves to each other, a promise which lasted for about a year. Then Pat met someone at work and without a second thought ended up in her bed. The cycle began all over again until they both received Christ as Lord and Savior and realized what the Word of God says about marriage and adultery. Until they were taught the Word, they both thought that adultery was a common, accepted way in marriage. Since that time, they have become committed to one another and to the Lord. They realized that the generational curses were passed down to them and that they needed to pray for their children's marriages, their grandchildrens' marriages and so on down the generational lineage. They also realized that it takes the Word and a commitment to God first, then to their spouse, to break these curses.

CURSE: Adultery

BLESSING: Purity and faithfulness

SCRIPTURE:

Blessed are the pure in heart, for they shall see God.
—MATTHEW 5:8

PRAYER:

*Father, in the name of Your Son, Jesus, I thank You that
I have a pure heart, so that I may see You and know You.
I desire to be blessed and I desire that my heart and my
marriage will be pure and holy before You. Amen.*

SCRIPTURE:

Do you not know that the unrighteous will not
inherit the kingdom of God? Do not be deceived.
Neither fornicators, nor idolators, nor adulterers,
nor homosexuals, nor sodomites, nor thieves, nor
covetous, nor drunkards, nor revilers, nor extor-
tioners will inherit the kingdom of God.
—1 CORINTHIANS 6:9–10

PRAYER:

*Father, in the name of Your Son, Jesus, I break any gener-
ational curse of adultery that is in my family and any of the
generations before my marriage and after my marriage. I
thank You that I will inherit the kingdom of God and that
my marriage will be righteous before You, Lord. I pray that
I will not be deceived and that I will have wisdom in every
situation regarding my marriage. I thank You for a righteous spouse and a pure and holy marriage. Amen.*

Problems in Marriage

Scripture:

> Whoever commits adultery with a woman lacks understanding; he who does so destroys his own soul.
>
> —Proverbs 6:32

Prayer:

Father, in the name of Your Son, Jesus, I thank You that my soul will prosper and not be destroyed; therefore I will remain faithful in my marriage at all times. I break any curses that may have been in the generations before me in regard to adultery or unfaithfulness in marriage. My marriage will be glorifying to You, Lord, at all times. Amen.

Scripture:

> And God spoke all these words, saying…"You shall not commit adultery."
>
> —Exodus 20:1, 14

Prayer:

Father, in the name of Your Son, Jesus, I will obey Your Word that I shall not commit adultery. I thank You for making me pure and holy and that my actions will line up with Your Word at all times regarding my marriage. Amen.

Curse: Divorce

LIFE EXAMPLE: Jessica's parents were married until she was twelve years old. She remembers them arguing a lot prior to their divorce and almost felt a sense of relief when they decided to separate and ultimately divorce. Her mother got full custody and Jessica visited her dad every other weekend and for half of the summer vacation. Her parents did not speak to each other, so when it was time for Jessica to go to her dad's,

25

her mom would go to her room when he came to pick her up and drop her off. Jessica was being taught that to deal with problems you either hide or leave. At eighteen years of age, Jessica met a young man whom she later married at the age of twenty-one. They seemed to be happy for several years. Soon after their fifth anniversary, she found out she was pregnant with their first child. She gave birth on November 1 and by Thanksgiving they were arguing every day about everything from money to how to put on the toothpaste cap. The tension in their home had increased dramatically and Jessica's solution to this tension was to leave for several days at a time without telling her husband where she was going. By Christmas, Jessica had filed for divorce. After three years of being a single mom, Jessica began to get Christian counseling for her loneliness. She discovered that there was a generational curse of divorce in their family line. Not only had her parents divorced, but her grandparents and great-grandparents had also been divorced. Jessica made a decision to break the curse over her daughter, so the iniquity would be broken at her generation and all future generations. She prayed first to receive Christ as her personal Savior and then prayed God's Word regarding divorce and the marriage covenant. She is now married to her previous husband and they are expecting their second child.

CURSE: Divorce

BLESSING: Unity and commitment in marriage

SCRIPTURE:

> The Pharisees also came to Him, testing Him, and saying to Him, "Is it lawful for a man to divorce his wife for just any reason?" And He answered and said to them, "Have you not read that He who made them at the beginning 'made them male and female,' and said, 'For this reason a man shall leave his father and mother and be joined to his wife, and the two shall become one flesh'? So then, they are

no longer two but one flesh. Therefore what God has joined together, let not man separate."

—MATTHEW 19:3–6

PRAYER (for the single person):

Father, in the name of Your Son, Jesus, I believe Your Word that when I get married I am one with my spouse, therefore no person or circumstance can cause us to become two. I believe that any generational curse of divorce that has come down from previous generations is broken and that beginning with my spouse and me, no divorce will occur in our generation or our children's generation or any future generations. I thank You, Lord that what You have joined together cannot be separated. No matter what it looks like, Lord, I stand on Your Word as truth in my marriage and my life. Amen.

SCRIPTURE:

Now to the married I command, yet not I but the Lord: A wife is not to depart from her husband. But even if she does depart, let her remain unmarried or be reconciled to her husband. And a husband is not to divorce his wife.

—1 CORINTHIANS 7:10–11

PRAYER (for the married couple):

Father, in the name of Your Son, Jesus, we will follow Your Word that commands us not to divorce. We break any curse of divorce that has come down from past generations to our generation and to future generations. We will build a marriage of commitment and we will obey Your Word with regard to our marriage. We thank You, Lord for helping us understand one another and work out our differences so that we may have a marriage that exemplifies You, Lord. Amen.

SCRIPTURE:

He who finds a wife finds a good thing, and obtains favor from the LORD.

—PROVERBS 18:22

PRAYER (for the husband):

Father, in the name of Your Son, Jesus, I thank You that Your Word says that if I find a wife I have found a good thing. I thank You for Your favor and that my marriage will be edifying to You. I thank You that all the curses of divorce are broken at my marriage and no future generations will be plagued with this curse. I thank You, Lord, that my marriage is centered on You and Your unfailing word. Amen.

SCRIPTURE:

And the Lord God said, "It is not good that man should be alone; I will make him a helper comparable to him."

—GENESIS 2:18

PRAYER (for the wife):

Father, in the name of Your Son, Jesus, I thank You for my husband. Your Word states that I am to be a helper for my husband, so I plead the blood of Jesus over my relationship with my husband, and I ask You to help me be the helper that You designed me to be. I break any curse that may have come from any past generations that would deter me from fulfilling my role as my husband's helper. Thank You, Lord, for this marriage, and I pray that this relationship will be one that is glorifying and pleasing to You, Lord. Amen.

CHAPTER 4

Parent/Child Relationships

*C*URSE: Disrespecting your parents

LIFE EXAMPLE: I was raised in a home with two parents and an older brother and sister. My mother never had a lot of good things to say about her dad; therefore, I believe her disrespect for men was birthed in her relationship with her dad. This ultimately turned into a curse in our family. As far back as I can remember, we not only were disrespectful to my dad, but we were encouraged by my mom to be that way to him any chance we could get. I remember teasing him about his weight (when he was overweight). I remember always talking back and having a "smart" mouth to both of my parents. Instead of being disciplined, I was called "mouth." Until I received Christ, I did not realize how much I disrespected my parents. Then the curse tried to take hold of my children. My mom was visiting us, and she told my daughter to answer me in a disrespectful way when I told her to do something. My mom probably did not look at it as being disrespectful, but I know that my daughter did because later she told me she would never answer me that way. I have also seen this in the tone of one of my nieces when addressing her dad. He may ask her to do something, and she responds in a rude tone or says she will not do what he asks. I was astounded when I heard her because it reminded me so much of me when I was growing up. I believe a lot of this disrespect comes from the wives and how they treat their husbands and how they speak to them in front of the children. I have been reminded in my own marriage how important it is to pray the Word over this area of my life. If you struggle in this area, I pray that this personal story can help you be delivered from this curse and be blessed with the promises God is trying to bestow on us, if only we would receive them.

CURSE: Disrespecting your parents

BLESSING: An honoring relationship with your parents and receiving honor from your children

SCRIPTURE:

> Children, obey your parents in the Lord, for this is right. "Honor your father and mother," which is the first commandment with promise: "that it may be well with you and you may live long on the earth."
> —EPHESIANS 6:1–3

PRAYER:

> *Father, in the name of Your Son, Jesus, I thank You for breaking the curse of my disrespect toward my parents and the disrespect shown by generations before me toward their parents so that my children, their children and their children's children will not have to suffer under this*

curse. I thank You that Your Word says if my children honor me, they are promised long life and that things will go well with them. I pray that they would honor Your Word in this area of life. Give them the desire to do what is right before You, O Lord. Amen.

SCRIPTURE:

Children, obey your parents in all things, for this is well pleasing to the Lord.

—COLOSSIANS 3:20

PRAYER:

Father, in the name of Your Son, Jesus, I thank You for Your Word and that You have commanded our children to be obedient to us. Your Word breaks the curse over my family regarding disrespect and disobedience to us as parents, and it teaches our children how to please You. I break the generational curse of disrespect in my family, all the generations before me and all those ahead of me. Thank You, Lord, that I have the power through Jesus' name to bind this area of my life forever and ever. Amen.

SCRIPTURE:

Honor your father and your mother, that your days may be long upon the land which the LORD your God is giving you.

—EXODUS 20:12

PRAYER:

Father, in the name of Your Son, Jesus, I thank You that Your commandments are true to this day and that I will follow them until the end of my days. I thank You for teaching my children and me how we can receive long life and Your blessings. I break any curse of dishonor and disrespect in any of the relationships in my family, in my children's families and any future families that will be developed in my family line. I believe and receive Your Word from Genesis to Revelation, for it is life to my family and me. Amen.

CURSE: Believing that children are an inconvenience

LIFE EXAMPLE: When I first met my husband I had a discussion with him about how many children I wanted—two. There were many reasons I planned to have two children. One was that I had a plan for my life and did not want children to get in the way of that (I was not saved yet). I also did not want the responsibility that went along with more than two children. At that time I looked at children as an inconvenience. Since then, I have had a huge transformation and the Lord has promised us five children. I have a peace concerning this because I know that the Word of God will do as it says, that God will not give me more than I can handle. We can go back many generations in my family and find that they also believed that more than two or three children would be a huge inconvenience, so I needed to pray that this curse would be broken in my family and in my children's families.

CURSE: Belief that children are an inconvenience

BLESSING: Belief that children are a blessing from God

SCRIPTURE:

> Behold, children are a heritage from the LORD, the fruit of the womb is a reward. Like arrows in the hand of a warrior, so are the children of one's youth. Happy is the man who has his quiver full of them.
>
> —PSALM 127:3–5

32

PRAYER:

Father, in the name of Your Son, Jesus, I thank You for my children and the ones to come. Thank You, Lord, that they are a heritage from You. Thank You that I am called blessed if I have a quiver full of them. Lord, I break the curse, in the name of Jesus, over the generations before me that believed that children were an inconvenience or a nuisance. I thank You, Lord, for giving me the wisdom on how to raise them to become men and women who live to serve You. Amen.

SCRIPTURE:

So Abraham prayed to God; and God healed Abimelech, his wife, and his female servants. Then they bore children; for the LORD had closed up all the wombs of the house of Abimelech because of Sarah, Abraham's wife.

—GENESIS 20:17–18

PRAYER:

Father, in the name of Your Son, Jesus, I thank You for making my/my wife's womb an open womb to bear children, for I know that children are a blessing or You would not have closed wombs to curse the house of Abimelech. I thank You, Lord, for giving me children who can honor and give glory to You. Amen.

CURSE: Abortion

LIFE EXAMPLE: Susan was in her first year of college when she found out she was pregnant. She built up her nerve to tell her mom, who encouraged her to have an abortion. Her mother never thought twice about the abortion and never asked Susan if she wanted to have the baby and either raise or put the child up for adoption. The same month that Susan had become pregnant, her sister also came home with the news that she was pregnant. Her mom also told her to have an abortion. Two babies in one month were killed because Susan's mom was carrying a generational curse from her family line. When Susan's mom was sixteen, she also had had an abortion after her mother strongly encouraged her to do so. This curse was not broken until Susan came to know the Lord and understand that His will is life, not death. Now Susan ministers to other women who are pregnant and considering their options, helping them understand that life is a choice that God blesses.

CURSE: Abortion

BLESSING: Life and the ability to bear children

SCRIPTURE especially for those who have had an abortion:

> If we confess our sins, He is faithful and just to forgive us our sins and to cleanse us from all unrighteousness.
>
> —1 JOHN 1:9

PRAYER:

> *Father, in the name of Your Son, Jesus, thank You for Your faithfulness to forgive my sins. I confess that I have willfully taken a life that You blessed me with. Thank You for forgiving me and cleansing me from all unrighteousness. I thank You for breaking the generational curse of death in my family, my children's family and their children's family. I believe and receive life and all the blessings that come with it. Amen.*

SCRIPTURE:

I praise You because I am fearfully and wonderfully

made; your works are wonderful, I know that full
well. My frame was not hidden from you when I was
made in the secret place. When I was woven
together in the depths of the earth, your eyes saw my
unformed body. All the days ordained for me were
written in your book before one of them came to be.

—Psalm 139:14–16, niv

Prayer:

*Father, in the name of Your Son, Jesus, I thank You and
praise You for creating me and ordaining my life and my
days on this earth before I was even born. Thank You,
Lord, for breaking any curses of abortion and death that
may be in the generations before me and the generations
that follow. Thank You that any child that is created is
fearfully and wonderfully made, and my family and my
children's families will always choose life. Amen.*

Scripture:

Before I formed you in the womb I knew you;
before you were born I sanctified you; I ordained
you a prophet to the nations.

—Jeremiah 1:5

Prayer:

*Father, in the name of Your Son, Jesus, I thank You that
You knew me before I was formed in my mother's womb
and that You have already ordained my destiny. I thank
You for breaking any curse of abortion or death in the
generations before me and those to come. I thank You for
all my children, and I commit to raise them according to
Your Word and Your will. Amen.*

CHAPTER 5

Laziness and Poverty

CURSE: Laziness and lack of motivation

LIFE EXAMPLE: Laziness can cause many disputes in a marriage and much frustration as a parent. Patty grew up in a home with a dad who never helped around the house. Patty's mom had to do all the household duties as well as work a full-time job. When she arrived home at night, she would find her husband, who was unemployed for over two years due to lack of desire to find a job, watching television. There would be no dinner cooked and no laundry done, and the house would be a mess. Patty's brother, Joe, did not help with the chores because he watched how his dad never did anything to help. Joe dropped out of school in tenth grade and stayed home with his dad. When Joe was seventeen he moved into an apartment with his girlfriend. She worked and Joe stayed at home. Do you see the pattern? This is the curse that has been passed down from one generation to the next; it can result in many difficulties in relationships and hinder success in employment and school.

CURSE: Laziness and lack of motivation

BLESSING: Abundance of energy and ability to accomplish things

SCRIPTURE:

> He gives power to the weak, and to those who have no might He increases strength. Even the youths shall faint and be weary, and the young men shall utterly fall, but those who wait on the LORD shall renew their strength; they shall mount up with wings like eagles, they shall run and not be weary, they shall walk and not faint.
>
> —ISAIAH 40:29–31

PRAYER:

> *Father, in the name of Your Son, Jesus, I thank You for the power that You give me that strengthens me. I break the curse of laziness that has been passed down from past generations to me and my children. I thank You, Lord, that when I wait on You, my strength shall be renewed. I will run and not be weary and I will walk and not faint because I wait on You, Lord. Amen.*

SCRIPTURE:

> He who is slothful in his work is a brother to him who is a great destroyer.
>
> —PROVERBS 18:9

PRAYER:

Father, in the name of Your Son, Jesus, I know that Your Word says that if I am slothful, I am joined with the enemy. I ask You Lord to remove any laziness in me or in my children. Thank You for abundant energy and motivation, and may all that I do be for Your glory. Amen.

SCRIPTURE:

Laziness casts one into a deep sleep, and an idle person will suffer hunger.

—PROVERBS 19:15

PRAYER:

Father, in the name of Your Son, Jesus, I thank You for removing any laziness that has been passed down from the previous generations in my family. Your Word states that if I am lazy and idle, I will go hungry. I thank You Lord for giving me motivation to work and complete all the tasks that You have set before me. I bind any lazy spirit from attaching itself to me. Amen.

CURSE: Poverty and lack

LIFE EXAMPLE: Patrick was raised in a lower income neighborhood where his mom and dad struggled daily to meet the family's needs. He was told that they did not have enough money every time he asked for something like a toy or new shoes. His mom often cried at night because she wanted her children to have the things that she didn't while growing up. Her family also experienced lack, and she was raised in a one-bedroom house with four children. When Patrick was twenty-three, he ran into one of his high school buddies in a corner store. His friend had moved away four years ago but was home visiting for the holidays. He was dressed in an expensive suit and a nice pair of dress shoes. Patrick began to ask him how he was doing when Steve began to witness to him about what the Lord had done for him through the past two years of his life. He never once mentioned the wealth he had been blessed with, but he told Patrick about the peace and joy that the Lord had brought into his life. Patrick was so intrigued he asked Steve to come over to his apartment to talk some more. By the end of the evening, Patrick had prayed for Christ to enter his heart and rule over his life. Today, five years later, Patrick has peace and joy as well as prosperity and all the things God promises in His word. Patrick had to break the curse of poverty and lack in his family before he was freed from this curse. He also has had to learn to speak those things that the Word of God says and not the things he was taught to say in his family regarding finances.

CURSE: Poverty and lack

BLESSING: Prosperity and met needs

SCRIPTURE:

> This Book of the Law shall not depart from your mouth, but you shall meditate in it day and night, that you may observe to do according to all that is written in it. For then you will make your way prosperous, and then you will have good success.
> —JOSHUA 1:8

PRAYER:

> *Father, in the name of Your Son, Jesus, I thank You for Your Word that I can meditate in it day and night and observe all that is written in it, making my way prosperous. In the name of Jesus, I break the generational curse of poverty and lack from the generations before me, in my family and in the generations to follow me. Thank*

You Lord for prosperity and wealth and for meeting all my needs and all my children's needs. Amen.

SCRIPTURE:

And my God shall supply all your need according to His riches in glory by Christ Jesus.

—PHILIPPIANS 4:19

PRAYER:

Father, in the name of Your Son, Jesus, I thank You for supplying all my need according to Your riches and glory by Christ Jesus. I thank You that all my needs are met and I lack no good thing. Thank You, Lord, for breaking the generational curse of lack and poverty in my family. Thank You, Lord, that I will never be broke another day of my life. Amen.

SCRIPTURE:

Beware that you do not forget the LORD your God by not keeping His commandments, His judgments, and His statutes which I command you today, lest—when you have eaten and are full, and have built beautiful houses and dwell in them; and when your herds and your flocks multiply, and your silver and your gold are multiplied, and all that you have is multiplied...And you shall remember the LORD your God, for it is He who gives you power to get wealth, that He may establish His covenant which He swore to your fathers, as it is this day.

—DEUTERONOMY 8:11–13, 18

PRAYER:

Father, in the name of Your Son, Jesus, I thank You that You have given me the power to get wealth and that I am a partaker of Your covenant that was sworn to Abraham, Isaac and Jacob. I thank You, Lord, for breaking the curse of poverty and lack in my family, my children's families and their children's families. Thank You, Lord, that as I keep Your commandments and statutes, I can lay hold of my inheritance. Amen.

CHAPTER 6

Addictions and Illness

*C*URSE: Drug and alcohol addiction

LIFE EXAMPLE: My educational background is in chemical dependency, and in the prison we see many men and women who have committed crimes as a result of their addictions. This curse can be passed down many generations, but it is also a lie from the enemy that just because your mom or dad was an addict means you will be one too. I have seen belief in that lie actually cause people to use drugs and alcohol. They believe they are predestined for addiction, so they set themselves up to become addicts. Let me use Sue as an example. Sue's dad was an alcoholic, and her mom used marijuana in the home. When Sue turned thirteen, her mom introduced her to marijuana. She continued to get high with her mom until she was nineteen. She never thought it was wrong to get high with her parents because that is what she learned in her home. At age nineteen she was arrested for possession of crack cocaine. She had been dealing for four years to support her drug habit. Currently she is in prison serving a two-year sentence. Prior to confessing Christ as her Savior, Sue believed she couldn't quit using marijuana because her mom and dad have always used drugs and alcohol as a regular part of each day. She believed the lie that since her parents were addicts, she had no choice but to be an addict too. Sue now knows there is life without drugs and alcohol, and her daughter does not have to be raised the way she was.

CURSE: Drug and alcohol addiction

BLESSING: Sober and healthy mind, body and soul

SCRIPTURE:

> Do you not know that your body is the temple of the Holy Spirit who is in you, whom you have from God, and you are not your own? For you were bought at a price; therefore glorify God in your body and in your spirit, which are God's.
> —1 CORINTHIANS 6:19–20

PRAYER:

> *Father, in the name of Your Son, Jesus, I thank You that my body is not my own, but it is Yours; therefore, I will not put any unclean thing in it. This includes drugs or alcohol. I break any curse of drug addiction in any generations before me and any generations in the future. My children will be sober and drug free. My children's children will be sober and drug free, and their children will also be sober and drug free. I dedicate my body, this temple of the Holy Spirit to You, Lord. Amen.*

Scripture:

> I beseech you therefore, brethren, by the mercies of God, that you present your bodies a living sacrifice, holy, acceptable to God, which is your reasonable service. And do not be conformed to this world, but be transformed by the renewing of your mind, that you may prove what is that good and acceptable and perfect will of God.
>
> —Romans 12:1–2

Prayer:

> *Father, in the name of Your Son, Jesus, I thank You for breaking the curse of alcohol and drug addiction in my family. Thank You for breaking the curse from generations before me, my children's generation, their children's generation, and any generations after them. Thank You that Your Word says that I do not have to be conformed to this world and that I can be transformed by renewing my mind. I claim that my mind is renewed and nothing will stop me from following Your perfect will. Thank you for the ability to be sober and that I can present my body as a living sacrifice to You, Lord. Amen.*

Scripture:

> No temptation has overtaken you except such as is common to man; but God is faithful, who will not allow you to be tempted beyond what you are able, but with the temptation will also make the way of escape, that you may be able to bear it.
>
> —1 Corinthians 10:13

Prayer:

> *Father, in the name of Your Son, Jesus, I thank You for Your faithfulness to me that You will not allow me to be*

tempted beyond what I am able. Thank You that You have delivered me from any drug or alcohol use and that I can bear any temptation You may allow. Thank You for breaking any generational curse of drug or alcohol addiction in my family line and thank You that I can be sober and free from any peer pressure that may come my way. Your Word states that You will make the way of escape from any temptations that I cannot bear. Thank You for freedom in You, Lord. Amen.

CURSE: Sickness

LIFE EXAMPLE: Rhonda missed five weeks of work this year due to sickness. Her ailments ran anywhere from migraines to strep throat. She often complained about how she felt to her family and her coworkers. Rhonda grew up with a sister who also had many different illnesses while she was growing up, but she began attending a church when she was in college that taught the healing promises of God. When Rhonda would call her sister about her sicknesses, her sister would encourage her to pray and receive the healing that God promises in His Word. Rhonda didn't understand how God could heal her, so she continued to speak illness over her life; therefore, she continued to have illness in her life. Two months ago, Rhonda decided to go to church with her sister. She happened to go when the pastor was teaching on healing, and he passed out scriptures that related to healing. She took the list home and confessed those scriptures daily for two months. Rhonda has not had a migraine or any other illness since she began to speak God's Word over her life. Now she is teaching her children about the promises of God, and they have been released from the curse of sickness in their lives. Many of us live with sickness because we have not used the tools that God has given us in His Word. I pray that this testimony will change your perspective on God's Word and His promises for your life.

CURSE: Sickness

BLESSING: Perfect health

SCRIPTURE:

"For I will restore health to you and heal you of your wounds," says the LORD.

—JEREMIAH 30:17

PRAYER:

Father, in the name of Your Son, Jesus, I thank You for restoring my health and healing my wounds. Thank You, Lord, for breaking the generational curse of sickness in my family. I believe that You can heal me and my family and that our bodies will function in the perfection that You created them to function. Amen.

SCRIPTURE:

...who Himself bore our sins in His own body on the tree, that we, having died to sins, might live for righteousness—by whose stripes you were healed.

—1 PETER 2:24

PRAYER:

Father, in the name of Your Son, Jesus, I thank You for Your Son who died so that I may live in perfect health. Thank You, Lord, for breaking the curse of sickness from the generations before me and the generations to follow me. Thank You, Lord, for each stripe that Jesus took for me and my family's health and wellness. Amen.

SCRIPTURE:

And the tongue is a fire, a world of iniquity. The

tongue is so set among our members that it defiles the whole body, and sets on fire the course of nature; and it is set on fire by hell. For every kind of beast and bird, of reptile and creature of the sea, is tamed and has been tamed by mankind. But no man can tame the tongue. It is an unruly evil, full of deadly poison. With it we bless our God and Father, and with it we curse men, who have been made in the similitude of God. Out of the same mouth proceed blessing and cursing. My brethren, these things ought not to be so.

—JAMES 3:6–10

PRAYER:

Father, in the name of Your Son, Jesus, I thank You for healing my body and breaking the curse of sickness in my family and in my life. I will speak healing with my tongue at all times. I believe and receive that my body functions in the perfection in which You created it to function. Thank You, Lord, for breaking the curse of speaking illness and death in my family. I believe that I can choose life or death, and I choose life and wellness. Amen.

Chapter 7

Dissensions

CURSE: Constant arguing

LIFE EXAMPLE: Melanie grew up in a house full of constant arguing. Her mom would raise her voice whenever she got upset with Melanie's dad, so arguments behind closed doors didn't do much good. Melanie heard it all. She would lay awake at night wishing they would stop so she could sleep. This constant arguing continued until Melanie left home at age sixteen. She left because she could not handle living in that atmosphere any longer. When Melanie met Jeff, she thought he would be the answer to all her problems. She moved in with him and his parents and lived there for two years. They seemed like the perfect family. There was no arguing in their house. Everyone got along great. Jeff and Melanie decided to get married and move into their own apartment. After a couple of months, Melanie found herself yelling at Jeff about little things. She would find things that would irritate him and spitefully do those things just to upset him. This would provoke an argument, and they would yell back and forth until someone would give in and apologize. Jeff usually was the one to give in. He grew up with peace and quiet and was unsure how to handle this type of arguing. The arguing continued for a year. After this, Jeff decided he could not handle living with such strife, so he moved back home with his parents. Melanie could not understand why he moved out. She had to look back on how she felt in her home and begin to understand why it was so difficult for Jeff to put up with constant arguing. She even realized that when she opened her mouth to yell, she sounded just like her mother. Although she had said she would never end up like her, she had become just like her in this particular way. Jeff and Melanie eventually went to marriage counseling and are working on breaking the curses that seeped into their marriage before children enter the picture.

CURSE: Constant arguing

BLESSING: Peace and agreement

SCRIPTURE:

> But the wisdom that is from above is first pure, then peaceable, gentle, willing to yield, full of mercy and good fruits, without partiality and without hypocrisy. Now the fruit of righteousness is sown in peace by those who make peace.
>
> —JAMES 3: 17–18

PRAYER:

> *Father, in the name of Your Son, Jesus, I thank You that the curse of arguing handed down from previous generations is broken. I thank You for the fruit of*

righteousness that is promised to my family because we are peaceful. I thank You that the words that come out of my mouth are peaceful. Amen.

Scripture:

Let your gentleness be known to all men. The Lord is at hand. Be anxious for nothing, but in everything by prayer and supplication, with thanksgiving, let your requests be made known to God; and the peace of God, which surpasses all understanding, will guard your hearts and minds through Christ Jesus.

—Philippians 4:5–7

Prayer:

Father, in the name of Your Son, Jesus, thank You that I can be gentle and not argumentative. Thank You for the peace that surpasses all understanding through Christ Jesus. I break the curse of constant arguing that has been passed down from previous generations. I release gentleness, peace and love in my home and in my relationships with others. Thank You, Lord. Amen.

Scripture:

Live joyfully with the wife whom you love all the days of your vain life which He has given you under the sun, all your days of vanity.

—Ecclesiastes 9:9

Prayer:

Father, in the name of Your son, Jesus, I thank You that I can live joyfully with my spouse as you have commanded. I thank You for joy to replace the arguing in our relationship. I thank You that the curse of constant arguing is broken from the past generations and will not be carried on to the future generations of my children and my children's children. Amen.

CURSE: Bitterness and unforgiveness

LIFE EXAMPLE: For eight years, my husband and I have been teaching parenting classes in the prisons in Minnesota. Needless to say, we have seen some pretty devastating cases of bitterness and unforgiveness that have led these men and women into a life of crime and ultimately prison. One particular lady by the name of Kate stands out in my mind. Kate's father sexually abused her as a child, and her mom knew about it but ignored it. When Kate was a young teen, she began to get into trouble in school and use drugs. She also started to show signs of rage and uncontrollable behavior. By the time she was fifteen, she was locked up in juvenile detention more than a handful of times. Her parents would bail her out, but as soon as she came home, she would run away again. This cycle went on until Kate became pregnant at age seventeen. After having her daughter, she dropped out of school to raise her. She then began to use crack cocaine to help her deal with recurring dreams of her father's abuse. This only made matters worse. She became a prostitute to support her habit. This seemed easy for her because she had learned at a young age how to block out what was happening and think of other things, almost like being in the moment physically but not emotionally. Unfortunately for Kate, she hadn't realized how much bitterness and unforgiveness had built up inside of her. One night she had a flashback of her father's abuse while she was with a "customer" and she grabbed a knife and killed him. She didn't realize what she had done until she returned home and still had the knife in her hand. Her mother found her sobbing in the bathroom and called the police. Kate is now serving a sentence of thirty years. She began working on her past in prison and has realized that bitterness and unforgiveness can lead to death, not just physical death, but emotional and spiritual death. If Kate does not forgive herself and then her parents, she will never truly be able to receive God's forgiveness.

CURSE: Bitterness and unforgiveness

BLESSING: Joy and God's forgiveness

SCRIPTURE:

Let all bitterness, wrath, anger, clamor, and evil speaking be put away from you, with all malice. And be kind to one another, tenderhearted, forgiving one another, even as God in Christ forgave you.

—EPHESIANS 4:31–32

PRAYER:

Father, in the name of Your Son, Jesus, I thank You that You have helped me to put away all bitterness and that I can be tenderhearted and forgive those who have wronged me because I have experienced Your forgiveness. Thank You, Lord, for breaking any curse of unforgiveness and bitterness that is in past generations of my family, our generation and in future generations. Thank You for giving me the peace that comes with letting go of bitterness and unforgiveness. Thank You, Lord, for the ultimate example of this in Your Son, Jesus. Amen.

SCRIPTURE:

But love your enemies, do good, and lend, hoping for nothing in return; and your reward will be great, and you will be sons of the Most High. For He is kind to the unthankful and evil. Therefore be merciful, just as your Father also is merciful.

—LUKE 6:35–36

PRAYER:

Father, in the name of Your Son, Jesus, I commit to loving my enemies and those who have done wrong to me. I want to follow in Your way, Lord, and I thank You for guiding and directing me by Your Word. Thank You for breaking the curse of unforgiveness in my family, in the generations before me and those to come after me. Thank You, Lord, for being merciful to me and teaching me how to be merciful to my enemies. Amen.

SCRIPTURE:

And whenever you stand praying, if you have anything against anyone, forgive him, that your Father in heaven may also forgive you your trespasses. But if do not forgive, neither will your Father in heaven forgive your trespasses.

—MARK 11:25–26

PRAYER:

Father, in the name of Your Son, Jesus, I break any generational curse of bitterness and unforgiveness that may have been in my grandparents' generations, my parents' generations or those that come after my generation. I commit to forgiving all those who have trespassed against me just as You have forgiven me for my trespasses. Thank You, Lord, for teaching me how to forgive and to receive Your forgiveness. Amen.

CURSE: Mishandling anger

LIFE EXAMPLE: Matt grew up in a home where the only emotion expressed was anger or rage. He witnessed a lot of yelling between his parents along with hitting and throwing objects, cursing and disrespect. The tragic event that left him in turmoil was when he witnessed his mom kill his grandfather. She went into an uncontrollable rage one night and pulled a gun on him and shot him. Matt will never forget the incident. Now that

Matt is eight, he has begun to show signs of the same uncontrollable rage that gripped others in his family. At home, he constantly throws objects when he does not get his way. At school, he kicks and screams when his teachers correct him. He has been placed in a special school for children with emotional problems. He acts impulsively instead of stopping to think about how to react. Looking back, we can trace down to three generations in Matt's family where anger was mishandled. His grandmother was raised in a violent home and constantly yelled at his mom while growing up, and his mom's most often expressed emotion is anger. The only true solution to this generational curse is the Word and prayer. The blessing that this family needs to believe for is peace and an appropriate expression of anger. Anger is a normal reaction to certain events, but it must be expressed in a productive, healthy way.

CURSE: Mishandling anger

BLESSING: Peace and the appropriate expression of anger

SCRIPTURE:

A fool gives full vent to his anger, but a wise man keeps himself under control.

—PROVERBS 29:11, NIV

PRAYER:

Father, in the name of Your Son, Jesus, I thank You for making me a wise person who keeps my emotions under control. I break any curse of rage or mishandling anger back to the third and fourth generations before mine and to the generations after me. Thank You, Lord, for giving me the wisdom to not act impulsively and to put my feelings under subjection to You and Your Word. I thank You, Lord, for peacefulness in my mind, body and soul from this day forward. Amen.

SCRIPTURE:

Let all bitterness, wrath, anger, clamor, and evil speaking be put away from you, with all malice. And be kind to one another, tenderhearted, forgiving one another, even as God in Christ forgave you.

—EPHESIANS 4:31–32

PRAYER:

Father, in the name of Your Son, Jesus, I thank You for Your word that instructs us to be kind to one another in the words that come out of our mouths. I pray that You would break any curse of rage or mishandling anger that has been in the previous generations in my family and those ahead of me. I will put away any anger with malice that tries to rear its ugly head in my relationships. I will operate in forgiveness and kindness and be tenderhearted toward those I come in contact with. Thank You for peace and joy in my life from this day forward. Amen.

SCRIPTURES:

So God created man in His own image; in the image of God He created him; male and female He created them.

—GENESIS 1:27

The LORD is merciful and gracious, slow to anger, and abounding in mercy.

—PSALM 103:8

PRAYER:

Father, in the name of Your Son, Jesus, I thank You that I have been created in Your image and You are a merciful and gracious God who is slow to anger. Therefore, I should be like You, slow to anger. Thank You, Lord, for giving me the ability to handle my anger appropriately and to continue to be more like You. Thank You, Lord, for peace and joy in my life and my children's lives and their children's lives. Thank You for breaking the curse of rage and mishandling anger that may have been in the generations before me. Thank You, Lord, for having mercy on me when I have mishandled anger in the past. Amen.

CHAPTER 8

Pride, Lack of Wisdom and Dishonesty

CURSE: Pride

LIFE EXAMPLE: James was raised by his mom and dad in a home that emphasized a strong work ethic, along with good values such as respecting authority, honesty, belief in God and having a vision. This all seems very important, but what James realized later in his life is that the curse of pride had been subtly woven into his life. One event in the family started James down the road toward deliverance from pride, and that was when James' dad called one day and told him his aunt was about to lose her house unless she received a certain amount of money. James asked his dad why she hadn't told them before it went into foreclosure status. His dad responded by saying, "You know that pride that runs in our family." When James heard that, he prayed against the curse that was on their family, but that didn't put an end to pride in his life—not yet. When James got married, and he and his wife began a ministry, he believed that if there were some challenges financially he should just pray and not ask other believers and supporters of the ministry to pray because that in some way meant that he didn't trust God. He continued down this path, and one day something happened that God used to uncover and break the curse of pride in his life. His wife had become pregnant with their fourth child. Many people knew of the good news because their quarterly newsletter had the announcement in it, and she had been at a large conference with many others that knew about her pregnancy, but in her eleventh week, their baby went to heaven. This event opened the door for James to let others know that he needed them and their prayers. This also opened the door for him to realize that others did not know about the financial challenges they had been facing for the past six months. He realized that other believers wanted to help and pray, but he would not let them know because of pride. It took this sad event for James to break the curse of pride and open himself up to the blessing of humility.

CURSE: Pride

BLESSING: Humility

SCRIPTURE:

> Likewise you younger people, submit yourselves to your elders. Yes, all of you be submissive to one another, and be clothed with humility, for "God resists the proud, but gives grace to the humble." Therefore humble yourselves under the mighty hand of God, that He may exalt you in due time.
> —1 PETER 5:5–6

Prayer:

Father, in the name of Your Son, Jesus, I break the curse of pride in my life and the generations before me and after me. Lord, thank You that Your Word says that if I have pride, You will resist me and that You give grace to the humble. I desire to be humble, Lord. Please show me when I allow pride to enter any area of my life. I desire to be clothed in humility and submit to one another as You have said in Your Word, and then You will exalt me in due time, Lord. Amen.

Scripture:

Therefore whoever humbles himself as this little child is the greatest in the kingdom of heaven.
—Matthew 18:4

Prayer:

Father, in the name of Your Son, Jesus, I thank You for giving me the spirit of humility like a little child so that I can come to You without pride in my heart. I thank You, Lord, for breaking any generational curse of pride that has flowed down from my parents, my grandparents, and any generations before them. I also use Your Word to break the curse of pride in my children's lives and their children's lives. I know that You desire a humble servant, and I desire to be this servant at all times. Thank You Lord for Your help in revealing any area of my life that may have pride in it. Amen.

Curse: Making bad choices/Lack of trust

Life example: My dad became a compulsive gambler before he and my mom got married. When she married him, she married into $15,000 worth of gambling debt, a very large amount of money at the time. She helped pay off this debt, and they remained married for the next twenty-seven years. He committed to quit gambling and attended Gamblers Anonymous. He ended his gambling but continued to be very irresponsible with money. He would not pay bills on time and would not tell my mom. The straw that broke the camel's back and their marriage was when my dad told my mom that he sold fake stock for money. He had run the risk of being arrested and imprisoned. By the grace of God, he did not have to endure punishment for this crime. My parents' marriage ended on very bitter terms, and he continues to be irresponsible with his choices regarding finances.

Seeing how making bad choices affected my parents' marriage, I had a hard time trusting my husband with the checkbook or paying bills. My brother went on in life to gamble and make some bad choices regarding his finances. Generational curses don't always result in the same behavior, and in my case, it resulted in a lack of trust. This lack of trust birthed from a bad role model could have destroyed my marriage like it did my parents'.

There are a couple of curses to break here. One is the curse of making bad choices. The other curse is the lack of trust. First we will address the blessing of making wise choices, then the trust blessing.

CURSE: Making bad choices

BLESSING: Making wise choices

SCRIPTURE:

> Therefore whoever hears these sayings of Mine, and does them, I will liken him to a wise man who built his house on the rock: and the rain descended, the floods came, and the winds blew and beat on that house; and it did not fall, for it was founded on the rock.
>
> —MATTHEW 7:24–25

Prayer:

Father, in the name of Your Son, Jesus, I pray that I will be like the wise man who built his house on a rock and that I will make wise choices for the remainder of my days. Thank You Lord for helping me make these wise choices in my life and in my marriage. Father, I break the curse of making bad choices and the lack of wisdom from the generations before me, in the name of Jesus, Amen.

Scripture:

See then that you walk circumspectly, not as fools but as wise, redeeming the time, because the days are evil. Therefore do not be unwise, but understand what the will of the Lord is.

—Ephesians 5:15–17

Prayer:

Father, in the name of Your Son, Jesus, I thank You for helping me walk circumspectly. Thank You for revealing Your will, Lord, that I may make wise choices that line up with what You want to do in my life. Amen.

Scripture:

Blessed is the man who walks not in the counsel of the ungodly, nor stands in the path of sinners, nor sits in the seat of the scornful; but his delight is in the law of the Lord, and in His law he meditates day and night.

—Psalm 1:1–2

Prayer:

Father, in the name of Your Son, Jesus, I thank You that I can be a person who does not take heed to ungodly counsel nor stands in the path of sinners, but that I can delight myself in Your law and meditate on it day and night so that I may make wise choices. Amen.

Curse: Lack of trust

Blessing: Trust

Scripture:

The God of my strength, in whom I will trust; my shield and the horn of my salvation, my stronghold and my refuge; my Savior, You save me from violence.

—2 Samuel 22:3

Prayer:

Father, in the name of Your Son, Jesus, I put my trust in You. You are my strength and my shield. I bind the generational curse of lack of trust in my family and the generations before me. I trust that You are my refuge and my stronghold. I believe that You will save me from violence and harm. Amen.

Scripture:

O Lord my God, in You I put my trust; save me from all those who persecute me; and deliver me.

—Psalm 7:1

Prayer:

Father, in the name of Your Son, Jesus, I put my trust in You and I believe that You will save me from those who persecute and use me. Thank You Lord. Amen.

Trust in the LORD with all your heart, and lean not on your own understanding; in all your ways acknowledge Him, and He shall direct your paths.

—PROVERBS 3:5–6

PRAYER:

Father, in the name of Your Son, Jesus, I believe that as I trust You, lean on You and acknowledge You, You will direct me down the right path. I bind the curse of mistrust that has plagued my family, and I release trust in the name of Jesus.

CURSE: Dishonesty

LIFE EXAMPLE: Mary learned to lie at an early age. Her mother was having an affair with another man and Mary found out. Her mother told her that she should not tell her dad about the affair or else she would be the reason that their marriage would be destroyed. Mary carried this burden most of her life until her dad found out about the affair for himself. Mary discovered that lying kept things calm and apparently peaceful in the home, so when she married her husband, she would lie about things if she thought he would get upset about the truth. She became so compulsive about her lies that she would have to lie to cover up her original lies. She eventually believed her own lies and could not discern the truth from a lie. When she began to have children, she discovered the curse that had been put on her and she began to seek counseling for her lying problem. She had to go back to her childhood to discover the root of the curse. She eventually discovered that lying was not the way to avoid problems, and to this day she tells the truth to her husband and children, even when it hurts. She also prayed to break the curse of dishonesty over her family and future generations. This is critical for moving ahead in a life of honesty.

CURSE: Dishonesty

BLESSING: Honesty

SCRIPTURE:

Lying lips are an abomination to the LORD, but those who deal truthfully are His delight.
—PROVERBS 12:22

PRAYER:

Father, in the name of Your Son, Jesus, I desire to be a delight to You, so please help me speak truthfully about everything. I thank You for binding the curse of dishonesty that may have been in the generations before me and I bind the curse of dishonesty in the next generations after me. I thank You that Your Word states that You hate lying, so I declare today that I will be honest in all my actions and words from this day forward. Amen.

SCRIPTURE:

Who may ascend into the hill of the LORD? Or who may stand in His holy place? He who has clean hands and a pure heart, who has not lifted up his soul to an idol, nor sworn deceitfully. He shall receive blessing from the LORD, and righteousness from the God of his salvation.
—PSALM 24:3–5

PRAYER:

Father, in the name of Your Son, Jesus, I thank You for Your promise that if I live life honestly and with a pure heart that follows after You, I will receive blessings from You and can stand in Your holy place. I desire this more than anything, Lord, so I bind the generational curses of lying and deceitfulness that may have been in the generations before me and may be passed to the generations to come. I thank You that I can live an honest life and the words that come out of my mouth will only be ones that are honest and pleasing to You, Lord. Thank You, Lord, for your grace and mercy for all the things I have said in the past that were not honest and thank You for giving me a pure heart that follows after You. Amen.

Conclusion

I have heard many times that the exit is more important than the entrance, so I would like to leave you with these final few words of encouragement.

Now that you have read about curses and blessings, I pray that you choose blessings. I know for a fact that God wants you to do so. He proves this in many ways. One example of how important blessings are to God is that in His Word, the words "bless," "blessings" and "blessed" are used almost three times as often as "curse," "cursed," or "curses."

In addition, His words through Moses state in Deuteronomy 30:19: "I call heaven and earth as witnesses today against you, that I have set before you life and death, blessing and cursing; therefore choose life, that both you and your descendants may live."

It's as simple as it sounds, and God has told us which to choose. I encourage you this day, now that you have prayed

66

over the curses that have bound up your life, choose life and blessings for yourself and for your family.

So often, we believe and speak that we are cursed. Well, I am in agreement with you as you choose to never again speak or receive curses over your life.

> *Father, in the name of Your Son, Jesus, I thank You for blessings and life more abundantly for the readers of this book and for their families. Thank You, Lord, that Your Word states that we can choose life and when we do, we and our descendants can live in joy and prosperity. Thank You, Lord, that all the curses that the reader has bound will never again show their faces in his or her life. I thank You, Lord, that the generations before them and the ones to come are blessed and that they will follow after You, Lord. Amen.*

To contact the author:
Lori Strong
Walking in Faith Ministries
7111 W. Broadway Ave., Suite 206
Brooklyn Park, MN 55428

Phone: (763) 503-2892
Email: pwp@youbetnet.net